# American Pye

## Autobiography of a Cat

Eugenia Eberle

Copyright © 2023 by Eugenia Eberle

ISBN: 978-1-77883-001-3 (Paperback)

978-1-77883-002-0 (E-book)

All rights reserved. No part of this publication may be reproduced, distributed, or transmitted in any form or by any means, including photocopying, recording, or other electronic or mechanical methods, without the prior written permission of the publisher, except in the case brief quotations embodied in critical reviews and other noncommercial uses permitted by copyright law.

The views expressed in this book are solely those of the author and do not necessarily reflect the views of the publisher, and the publisher hereby disclaims any responsibility for them.

BookSide Press
877-741-8091
www.booksidepress.com
orders@booksidepress.com

Dedicated

to

Charlie

The coolest cat

# American Pye

## 20 August 82 - 6 December 99

Many years ago, when I was very young, I was given to a member of my new family as a birthday present. By being attentive, loving, passionate and gentle my master, Roik, brought me up in a very special way. Naturally small, with almond shaped cobalt blue eyes, I appeared helpless and vulnerable, and easily became his prize. There were times when he confided his treasured thoughts, that I was his "Sweet Pye" or some times in jest, "Darleeene," but because it is my nature to uphold a certain image, the family was apt to refer to me as "Princess." Actually, you see, my official name in the pedigree sense is "Saki" because I come from the Orient and fit into that very special breed, the Siamese. "Pye" was adopted later from a family name of Irish lineage, and that was precisely what I was called for the rest of my life.

Unfortunately, I had a healthy appetite for delectable morsels, which I was given generously. Consequently, in my later years, I found that I had a tendency to gain a bit of weight, but when I heard them refer to me as "beautiful", I was not one to argue the obvious. It was my great fortune on the other hand, to be able to disguise this extra fullness beneath my silky cream and chocolate-colored fur, for if they were to suspect such, they would surely have curbed those tidbits I so dearly loved every now and then.

Classified as a Seal Point Siamese, I was always fiercely devoted to ruling my roost and protecting any advantage overall. This meant keeping order in what was reasonably deemed general chaos. With this enormous responsibility as first feline of the homestead, a grand old place where there was both an abundance of animals and activity, I found that it was necessary to maintain a rather sensible routine, one that allowed me to miss nothing. There were times, however, when I would just as soon get away from it all, for life down on the farm had a tendency to be wearing at times.

One day, when I was about a year old, my master disappeared. For a time, he had made a greater fuss over me than was usual, but I had not suspected anything like his sudden departure. His absence bothered me for some time, and even though his family remained, all the while taking good care of me, I felt an empty spot in my heart for a long, long while. After what seemed like forever, he came back for a short visit and upon his arrival he asked of my whereabouts straight away. I know, because I just happened to be within hearing distance, and recognized his voice. Being coy and very feminine, I waited for him to find me, all the while pretending I hadn't heard. Suddenly, I was snatched from my snoozing position and squeezed tightly. His enormous smile shone down and I was simply beside myself. Had I been able to talk people-talk, I'm sure I'd have told him to "slow down, fella, I can't breathe!" We looked at one another for a long minute. His great, large eyes set within an open happy face, looked at me warmly, and as I tried to wriggle to gain my freedom, I realized he was not about to let me go. I began to listen to all the things he wanted to share with me and it was then that I learned he had left me behind because his lifestyle in the big, wide world would be difficult for me. We were both lucky to have the loving people at the homestead to watch over me during his absence. He would come and go for the rest of my life.

My family consisted of six: My master, of course; his parents, Missy and Hubby; his two brothers, Jedd and Fibby; and Rennie, their sister, who owned and spoiled three talking parrots.

After Roik moved away, Jedd and Fibby remained close at hand, living in separate spaces at the homestead. As they were grown young men about town, they were not on the premises a lot, but they were kind and attentive when they were here.

Having moved from Saudi Arabia to Albuquerque, my family wanted land their new town. When they found this old territorial-style homestead on three and a half acres in the north valley they immediately named it the DO OH DA AH Ranch from the fond memories of their recent adventure. Once occupied by the governor of New Mexico, it had a high, very heavy red-rock Spanish wall around the back garden area which enclosed the formal garden. A "secret garden" with an adobe bench or 'banco' was hidden in the corner behind large pruned junipers. Sometimes these bancos are double sided like the one in the open garden. We felines loved to gather around the nearby fish pool rimmed with multi-colored Italian tile to watch the carp, and were sometimes successful in caching one to share. A large cyclone fence surrounded the entire property where several old cottonwood trees shed their pollen every year, giving the air a look of floating cotton balls.

The front of the homestead was formal and the gate there in the cyclone fence was locked most of the time. As I remember, it was only opened occasionally for a large party, otherwise the lingering folk from the street might feel free to come in and look around. Within that gate was a raised adobe turnabout, a structure near the center of the gravel parking area big enough to park ten cars. In the structure were a few tall pines and a statue standing subtly in the trees. After parking, one would step up to a red tiled patio walk which approached a corbelled covered entryway. The handcrafted wooden front door that had a beautiful, small, wrought-iron latch that could be opened up to check who the guest might be. Along the extension of the wall from the front door, the patio continued to a small, grey southwest, rustic wooden door that we could crawl under to enter the inner garden. In front of the wall, were three beautiful square rose gardens and an old trumpet vine, hugging the wall, which Missy had pruned to resemble a medieval dragon. This brick area got too hot for our feet sometimes so we didn't spend much time out there.

The back entrance was less formal and lined with lilac bushes which took Missy two weeks to prune each year. Long adobe cottage or 'batch' as they called it, housed my master and me until he left. Guests would occasionally occupy those rooms later on.

When I heard that they bought the place as a "white elephant," I didn't understand the term. It was very difficult for me to think of white elephants living here on the property. Missy and Hubby apparently fell in love with the old place and thought it would be an adventure to restore it. Besides the cottage, there were corrals, and a stable, which meant there was a room for everyone. So one by one, they added to the growing menagerie.

The family was devoted to animals. I know, because we were all given time and assurance. Actually, when I arrived, there were already other animals here, so it took time to develop the superiority that was part of my nature. When Missy and Hubby moved in, there was already a cat there that greeted the family, probably left by previous owners. Known as "Souchi", this outdoor cat, a calico, and very low on our feline totem pole, was found perched in the crook of the roof above the back entrance as though standing guard. Missy had been a bit fearful of this very large calico that appeared to be dangerous by the way he/she sat so vigilantly, almost territorial by nature. One day, however, I saw a man come pick her up. I later learned that she was rare and wanted in another household with other calicos.

There were also two basset hounds on the premises. Missy had bought them as a surprise for Rennie when she returned from school. This colorful duo were from the same litter and raced about making noise and pretending they were more ferocious than they really ever could be. You see, they were mere puppies, just a few months older than I. These hounds were called Huuwah and Hiiyah, names that I thought were somewhat peculiar; oh, something to do with Arabic pronouns! Missy wanted to get a llama and call it Huum for Huumdelallama, which would finish the he-she-it part of the Arabic conjugation, but she never brought a llama to the DO OH DA AH Ranch. These bassets had very different personalities, and at times their energy could be triggered by runners, people walking their dogs, children passing by the back gate going to or from the middle school nearby, or at an occasional stranger coming through the gate. Even though I had gained my confidence around them, I thought it best to keep my distance, particularly from Hiiyah, but generally I learned to roam about on my own without much difficulty. Our chemistry simply didn't jive I guess, but frankly, I think they were just obnoxious and far too demanding.

Hiiyah was spayed. She made the mistake of breaking her leg only a few days before coming into her second heat. Because she was always doing silly things, Missy and Hubby were always furious with her. They had gone to a great deal of trouble to find the right stud for her but became impatient with her now. A blessing in disguise I thought, particularly after hearing that the basset hound population had suddenly reached the point of saturation and none of us wanted to be overrun with bassets. I wasn't sure I could stand anymore long ears anyway.

Huuwah was a more docile type with big eyes and a square frame. He was plagued with the achondroplastic deformation that stunted bones in dwarfs. He rocked as he ran on his short, twisted legs, and as much as he wanted to keep up with his athletic sister, it was difficult for him and usually fruitless. He did, however, have the sense to stay out of trouble; instead, he would sit back and watch his sister do wrong. It always seemed to me that he actually anticipated her lunacy, for he would stand still, as though at attention, absorbing the situation before sitting on his haunches, and slowly lowering himself down on his forepaws to watch in horror some of her undisciplined actions. He was the kind of dog one calls "man's best friend," one who enjoyed companionship without asking for anything in return.

Why, I can think of the multitude of times when someone was talking to Huuwah, leaning over to caress the very long ears, talking to him as one would a good friend, when out of the blue the old girl would appear from nowhere to demand the attention being given to Huuwah. He would grit his teeth on most such occasions and then produce a low, menacing growl that had a challenging business-like tone. I was always delighted to watch him stand his ground as he put Hiiyah in her place on occasion, turning to chase her off.

Plans were difficult to make on a day-to-day basis, but I learned to be as flexible as possible, considering all I had to keep my eye on; the order of comings and goings of people and animals. Why, it was enough to keep me on my toes quite constantly, for I too, as anyone else, had my preferences, for special things to do.

Missy had espaliered the tall cyclone fence with a thorny, red-berried Pyracantha bush to give the appearance of many arms reaching out to grasp the others all the way around the four corners to the back gate. I remember many a time when I sat under the old apple tree in the shade to watch her take the time to carefully prune these bushes, which became very large in five years. This enclosed the acreage, so unless you were small like me, no one could escape and no unwanted ones could get in.

In the spring, another group of animals were brought to the DO OH DA AH Ranch. Ten sheep were being delivered and taken to graze in the back forty. Hubby had put in an irrigation system to keep the fields nice and green, which made the herd happy. I remember Fibby going into the field once in a while and making a really disgusting mess. I could count by then and there was always one less sheep when he left. By the year's end, we had no sheep at all. Then, the next spring, another herd appeared. This time, a great beautiful ram was amongst them. I can remember his large, steely, clear blue eyes giving him the appearance of a true leader. Of course, he had his harem to himself, and so leader or not, he was in control, no doubt about it! I was amazed at his curly horns, which resembled twisted taffy.

Early one morning, I was wakened by some commotion outside. I saw that the back gate was already open, unusual at this time of the morning, allowing a car to rush into the driveway. Missy was also up, but the rest of the family was just rising. A lady got out hurriedly and knocked on the back door just off the kitchen to tell us that while she was taking her husband to the airport, she had seen the ram push open the gate, and with the entire herd behind him and was heading down Guadalupe Trail. The car backed up and continued on its way. I ran to the ledge on the window in Missy's study where, beyond my belief, I could see the tail end of the last sheep running down the trail.

The herd follows...

Of course, no one would listen to me, but the commotion was exciting. It was easy for me to merely sit there and watch.

Everyone missed their breakfast that morning. I didn't, but they did! Such helter-skelter! Everyone scattered in different directions, some with sticks; some with cars. Jedd's orange V-dub bug disappeared around the corner, lickety-split! People from everywhere tried to help corner the herd, which took several hours to do, but once they were all returned and back behind the gate, I could hear the family discussing a solution to prevent this from happening again. By the end of the following weekend, Hubby, Fibby and Jedd had constructed a new gate and a corral. They also built a small barn to store hay and feed with space for extra shelter for the animals during the harsher weather.

Though, as I have already said how exhausting the place could be, there were times when I truly loved watching the variety of activity here. Sometimes I felt like a surveying hawk. It was an interesting experience to be an innocent bystander. Every day I had something new to look forward to; I could depend on it! Watching the sheep became a new amusement for me. They lambed several times that spring but, unfortunately, it was discovered that this last lot of sheep had worms and Hubby and Missy were forced to have them destroyed.

It was during this time, I had come of an age when Missy thought it necessary to find me a companion of the opposite sex. After a long search, she brought home a handsome Blue Point, Siamese of course, with papers a mile long. He was quite dashing with large, gray eyes. Long, gangly, and already twice my size, he was but only half my age! We don't worry about these things in the animal world, you know. It took him a few days to feel comfortable, but in much of that time, he would hide under Rennie's big spool bed upstairs. I kept an eye on him and let him know I was around. Slowly, as he began to wander about more freely, I took it upon myself to offer him a tour of the homestead. At least a week passed before Missy took him to the clinic to have his shots and a general physical. Later that day, it was announced, within earshot that my new spouse could never give me kittens after all, and that was probably the reason he was given to us in the first place, because his original owner was well aware of it! "Chin," as he was called, arrived not only with papers, but a fancy kitty litter box and a jungle gym, something I had never seen before. The jungle gym, a contraption of wooden levels wrapped in pieces of carpet, quickly disappeared, but that box was first class and well used by our expanding feline society.

When Chin was found sterile, it was decided that I should be spayed, not to have kittens at all. Never to be a mother! After my operation I recovered quickly, and not ever realizing the life of a wayward cat, I really don't have the foggiest idea what I might have missed.

As Chin gained his confidence, he became a rather macho type who stalked the grounds as though he had business to tend to. I loved watching him because he had great style. When he wanted to go outdoors, he merely went to the door and waited. Once the door was opened, he would dart over the threshold. He loved the double-seated adobe banco in the back yard where he would perch on an upper arm to muse at the beautiful and protected world around him. I know he caught all the delectable critters to be found there, day and night, but I am now almost certain that he had far too-good a time, in his independent way, not to be a local lady killer. Sterile, my eye!

It wasn't long after that when I woke one early morning with a start. A new sound I didn't recognize had come to the ranch. I scampered to the windowsill to watch two large animals being ushered with harnesses to their stalls. Quickly referred to as "the Girls," they were the largest animals I'd ever seen. I returned to snuggle down in my warm and protected space, but not being able to settle down again, I returned to the windowsill to watch. The darker animal, who we would call "Shaella," was a very large, black mare, once a barrel champion, who could satisfy most any rider. The other creature, a dappled-gray. Appaloosa, later became a bit of a disaster. Bought for Rennie, it was discovered that "Sophie" had a nervous disorder in her hind-quarters which prevented her from having a sure footing, apparently not uncommon in Appaloosas. For some time, the family members rode both horses until Sophie began to trip. Not until there were several falls was it decided that the dangers did outweigh the joys of riding and the Appaloosa was forbidden. The 'black', however, was ridden quite frequently.

One day, Fibby came home with an idea. It seems that a friend of his had been working on a stud farm and, for a very special price, would breed our girls with a superstud from a long line of race horses. Preparations were made and schedules were organized around the readiness of the mares. I could sense a new excitement building up about the place, and then one day, the red horse trailer was brought around to the open driveway where the horses would be hopefully loaded.

The black became impossible. Five men were unable to coerce Shaella into the trailer. I sat high up on the hay loft to watch for I always positioned myself to have a bird's eye view in order to see and hear as much as possible. I well remember that particular incident was full of cussing and swearing. "She's a corker," one shouted. "Stubborn as a mule," said another. I thought that the problem with her was a past experience, perhaps one that stamped fear into her from bad handling by an impatient owner. Well, they all finally gave up and scattered in different directions. After it quieted down and all the helping hands were gone, I came down to sit by Missy as she sat on the adobe banco to contemplate. Knowing there wasn't much time to spare when there's breeding to be done, she stayed with me for only awhile before getting up to phone Hubby. She had come up with the idea that they could hire Gilbert, the handyman, who came occasionally to help Missy around the ranch. She was sure he could ride the black to the stud farm some forty-five miles away because he once alluded to the fact that he knew the territory well.

Early the next morning, we were all up waiting eagerly for Gilbert who appeared all smiles. I was always so amused with the way he handled the horses. He seemed right at home with them although he had a particular affection for Shaella and was looking forward to returning to his old stomping grounds with her. Missy packed a lunch and wrote a note to put into his pocket in case there were any questions asked along the way, or an emergency of any kind.

Gilbert was a small, quiet man who nearly always wore a plaid shirt. His cowboy hat appeared to be oversized, shrinking him further into the saddle, but it was necessary to shade him from the very hot sun. As he left at the gate, he appeared the size of a jockey in the saddle of this great black mare. We all waved goodbye and wished him luck as he disappeared out of sight. Whew! I, too disappeared, to one of my favorite hide-a-ways to rest after all the commotion.

Some while later, Missy and Rennie prepared the trailer by hitching it to the truck. As soon as Sophie was on board, we all said goodbye again, as we watched the little red cart take the bend at the corner; Sophie's long, gray Appaloosa tail swishing about over the back gate of the trailer. Rennie bustled about and then, too, left for school.

The day flew by. I guess it had to do with all the excitement. Dinnertime was nearing and the sun was beginning to slip down behind the hills. Missy was in the kitchen, so Chin and I meowed at the door. Noticing our plea, she let us in and then went back to her preparation. We jumped onto our feeding station at the sink and waited. This was a time when Chin and I would make fun and bat Our paws at each other. I had noticed out of the corner of my eye that Missy was getting ready to open "our" can, number two of tuna and liver, and invariably she would lean closer as she snapped it open practically under our noses to give us the full fresh aroma as it released its essence from the can. We would almost swoon, lick our lips, and do a jig while she added a spoonful to the Kibbs. She got a great deal of pleasure watching us rev up for meals, our favorite times of the day Of course. She'd get such a kick out of stimulating our appetites as well. Sometimes, however, before she could finish mixing our dinner, the phone would ring. Chin and I would sit there paying attention to her every move, patiently waiting for her to return. We didn't like to wait too long for meals for fear we'd starve to death if not fed on time.

It was custom that after dinner I would disappear to preen. Becoming so involved with my post-supper bathing, I would at times be totally unaware of what was happening around me. However, on this particular night I was interrupted as I heard Missy hang up the phone having just been informed that Shaella, the black mare, had not been delivered to the farm. Several minutes passed when the phone rang again. This time it was Gilbert, and from what I could gather, he was lost and could not go any further because the horse had become terrified of the lights and honking cars in motion. Poor dear, she's gone through so much and what a time to become emotional! It was apparent that Missy and Hubby had been presented with an urgent problem.

By the time Hubby arrived home after his long day at the hospital, Missy had put some dinner into some containers, including enough for Gilbert, found some old blankets, and packed some oats in a container for the mare. She began to relay the story, and before Hubby was able to sit down for a quick breather, they hurried out the door in search of Gilbert and the mare, stranded in the dark somewhere near Los Lunas south of Albuquerque. Fortunately, Missy had written down directions to where they had stopped on a piece of paper so they could be found.

It was hours before they returned. By then, I was on the end of the bed where I always slept at night. They talked about the next day and described the evening as quite a harrowing experience. From what I could gather, Gilbert had become lost. Evidently he confessed he had not been in that area for so long that it had become unfamiliar territory and Shaella was nervous by the occasional automobile lights that spooked her in the darkness. He decided that even though they were close to their final destination he had to stop his journey and was able to settle down in a small hay truck adjacent to a corral so that Our mare could spend the night close by.

The next morning, Missy left just after Hubby, nearly forgetting to feed us. She dashed out after our breakfast to meet Gilbert and Shaella at the stud farm. Later that day, she came home without Gilbert, so I suppose she had taken him home after his frightening ordeal.

We didn't see the black mare for several days until suddenly she returned and merely carried on with her day as before.

What a sweet horse she was. In her prime, she had apparently been an excellent barrel racer, quick on her feet, and with a gentle personality. It wasn't long before Sophie, the Appaloosa, returned as well.

Felines generally prefer nighttime activity. Chin was the night stalker, but I was the day time girl. When nearly four, I paid my dues, when I went out prowling. Life on the DO OH DA AH Ranch could be pretty routine and something must have gotten into me. Perhaps I needed an R and R. Missy didn't allow us out too late and would usually round us up just before the lights went out. Normally, I would hang about the doors midway through the evening when the dogs were taken to their corral, but on this particular evening, as my memory serves me, I honestly think my intentions were to run away, well, maybe.. perhaps to give the family a little scare.

The sun was dusking on the mountains, turning them watermelon red, Sandia red. The world, my world, was coming in for supper and no one knew where I was as I perched on a stump, contemplating my next move. I had lost my appetite as I considered what I might do to experience more exciting things like an adventure. I rose up, arched my back and stepped down to begin my journey. Oh, yes, I hesitated a few times along the way and began to reconsider, for my home life was rather cushy, and with all due respect, they just might miss me.

The moon was high and very full which stimulated me as I relished my independence. I progressed quite far from home and before I knew it I was in unfamiliar territory. The insects were noisy as they made their way through the grasses and I could hear the rodents scratching as they came up out of their holes. An occasional moth would dart above my head which excited me. I'd swat my paw upward to catch it off guard, jumping, jumping, nearly plummeting into a prickly bush, hoping to catch the nighttime morsel, but no such luck. There was little danger of snakes, but I knew that there was a porcupine in the area. One of the new mares had been struck on the nose when she presumably bent down to investigate the movement before her in a corner of the field.

The night had passed, and the sun was now edging up over the ridge of the Sandia's, casting a subtle glow. I had indeed been moving most of the night. Now tiring of my expedition, I realized I was lost. I was not an experienced traveler and became leery of my whereabouts. I felt delicate now and not too intelligent. 'Had I actually strayed too far from comfort? Oh dear, what should I do? I must get my wits about me; try to pull myself together!' I thought. Crouching down to rest, I pondered my dilemma. I sniffed the air as I'd hoped to get a whiff of something familiar, but to no avail. 'Where had I gone? What had I been thinking?' Horrified, I was overcome with fear when, as though an angel passed by, I recognized the honking of one of our neighbors' geese preparing with the local roosters to advertise the new dawn. It wasn't going to be easy to pass the geese unseen unless I moved slowly and carefully through the brush near the Rio Grande River, not too far from Guadalupe Trail. The Trail was really a country road with houses set back on large properties in the north valley near the big city of Albuquerque. Fortunately, it was still quiet this hour of the morning, but nevertheless, a danger. 'Was I home free? Just over to the woodpile and back in time for breakfast?' I thought. That should be easy enough!' The geese seemed to be too busy eating their grain, to pay any attention to me, though one did see me and began to advance. Fortunately, he was distracted by one of his many siblings and went back to pecking the morning manna. I was able to get to the trail and crossed it easily.

    The animals in the neighboring pasture were also beginning to rise, but during the night, the field had been heavily flooded by the ditch nearby, making it difficult for me to get across. 'If I could only get beyond the high waters of that field, I'd feel more secure.' The birds above began to swoop at anything moving, so it was necessary to conceal myself as I skirted the field. I moved with care around the house and to my great joy, saw at last, the fence of our back forty looming before me. The dogs next door were treacherous and always on guard. 'If it's early enough,' I thought, 'I might have been able to bypass them.' It appeared that the water had blocked the hole through which I had set out my journey last night. 'Am I trapped?' I thought. I began talking to myself, as I looked for another way home. Scrambling, I found a new passage through an old, wild rose bush, unattended for years. Slowly, I crept under the fence at the school, and into the training ring for the colts. I planned to crawl under the gate at the water trough, pass the large compost pile, and to the woodpile that had stood tall, but was now in a random state. 'Once I passed that,' I thought, 'I could squeeze under the wooden fence, pass Jedd's room, and appear at the kitchen door as though nothing had happened.' The school's side fence was easy. Passing the training ring and under the gate was a breeze, but reaching the top of the woodpile where I had often sat, I settled on my haunches a moment to catch my breath when something beneath me began to wobble. The logs had not been stacked, just thrown, and although my weight was diminutive, a slight move was enough to cause the wood to shift causing me to be pinned under a large log. I must have blacked out because when I came to, I was trapped and could only lie there. So little and reasonably weak under the heavy logs, I had no other choice but to try to pull away Oh, I was in serious trouble, all right. I mean I was behind a wall and therefore just beyond meowing distance even if someone would happen to come this way. Much to my added distress, it would be unusual for anyone to come to the woodpile this early; that I was certain of! They'd be calling, but I was just oh so close, yet too far away to be heard.

    I lay there in pain. With all my remaining energy, I mustered up enough force to finally tug my back leg free. I should have known better than to stop at the wood pile because it had grown considerably during the recent renovation. Thank heaven it was not raining or I would have been labeled a drowned cat ...if found! I knew I had probably broken my leg, now pounding with pain. I pondered as I looked at the wooden fence, the last barrier between safety and me. Slowly, I dragged myself along the barricade and managed to crawl under the gate and up the walk as far as Jedd's room where I found a warm spot in the morning sun against the adobe wall at the ceramic tiled steps.

    As I lay there basking in a drowsy state, the DO OH DA AH Ranch came alive with the clacking of chickens, and the crowing of roosters. The dogs became restless in their pen, not too far away, and I could hear the mares whinnying, but they would be satisfied for a while to forage in the fields. I'd wished that Missy would soon arrive to feed the chickens and hopefully look for me as well. Fortunately, the silly hounds had not been released from their pen, for they would have made matters far worse had they been on the prowl, noses down, for a possible new intriguing scent to become excited about. In near shock, I continued to rest in the warm sunlight, knowing full well I had crushed my leg as it hung down over the step near Jedd's doorway.

Jedd's room was a small extension on this old house, probably meant as the maid's quarters in the old days and very near a beautiful swimming pool where Chin and I sometimes sat. Jedd was a rather late riser so I had no reason to think that he would be tripping over me anytime soon.

It was a little later when I was wakened by some excitement. I became aware of Missy standing over me, overjoyed and calling the others as she stooped down to examine me. Apparently, an earlier search had been futile and my family had been at their wits' end. Jed and Rennie arrived with a warm towel to carefully bundle me up, making sure my leg was up high near my torso and well supported. There they were, caring more than I would have ever dreamed. While I was still protected in my 'nest', Missy carried me into the house to replace the towel with another warmed one. Numb as I was, I remember being put on her lap under the steering wheel and being driven off directly to the clinic where x-rays were taken.

The vet found that my leg was badly crushed, and the X-rays revealed that there was a fracture of my thigh bone. He said it was either surgery or heaven. Aghast, Missy and Rennie decided on surgery, of course. I remember them hugging me before leaving the vet's office. The next day, late in the afternoon, Missy picked me up. I knew I wasn't going anywhere for some time. My leg was a ghastly sight, shaven to the skin. 'Oh what would Chinny say?' I could recollect his wise, large, gray eyes, which were watching as we arrived. Missy put me gently on a soft mat she had arranged on the living room floor near a sunny window where I could maneuver easily and bask in the warm sunshine. My handsome Chinny appeared to observe my new, now hairless leg for which Missy and Hubby would receive a nice big bill to put in their files labeled CATS.

I remember being impatient with Chin the day before I left, but now I was happy he was there to keep me company as I recovered from my ordeal. I would hobble for a long while waiting patiently for my Seal Point colors to return to my leg. We would sit together for long periods of time in the sun before he wandered out for the night. In retrospect, I was really happy to be home again within the warmth of my loving family. It would take six months for me to recover fully, and by then, my master would surely return. After a few months with renewed pleasure and a certain amount of playfulness, I began to feel like my old self again. I gained back some of my weight, but was concerned about the strange color of the fur that grew back.

I realized Chin was getting a bit restless. He had always appeared to love a battle because I could see that 'tough' look in his eye every now and then, and I would know when he had either been in a fight or was going out to one. 'My, oh my, what can I do with such a guy,' I thought. It wasn't long before he was missing one full day and two nights, when our man about town arrived looking in very bad shape. One side of his neck resembled a skinned rabbit with a pretty nasty deep gash revealing the inner structure of his anatomy. His wound, open and bloody, was tended to immediately. Every day I would watch Chin get lifted up by Rennie who would clean his wound faithfully and give him warm milk to quiet him. Rennie would have made a wonderful veterinarian. Unfortunately, it was necessary to administer some medicine, which caused him to gag each time. It made me shiver just to watch. He was not feeling too well and began to lose weight. I kept an eye on him the best I could, for I was of course anxious for him to recover. He led such a strenuous life that he began to appear far older than his years.

Several weeks lapsed before his appetite began to return and it soon became evident that he was putting on a little weight.

Slowly he began to leave his crankiness behind to resume his normal personality, even though he continued to sleep most of the day in the sunny, large living room, reclining in the great Chippendale chair, leaning heavily on a beautiful new petit-point pillow Missy had just finished. I decided that it was time for me to move my naptime from my favorite place in the dining room to the living room where I could keep some sort of vigilance on my dear one during his convalescence. Although it wasn't easy to change my own pattern, I knew he liked my company and would appreciate my being there with him.

      Each day Missy would pay him several visits just to keep an eye on him. She would either coax him to eat or just give him some TLC to coax him to purr a little, for that always helps in our healing, particularly when we are down and out. I remember one particular day when it was raining. I sensed that Chin was lingering longer than usual. Missy appeared and bent down quite close to check his breathing. He was really logy, so she gently began to move him enough to get his blood circulating when her eyes grew wide with horror. Her new pillow was covered with old, dried blood oozing from his wound The seat of the chair had also signs of this now-dried substance from another day. She carefully lifted Chin, who was extremely limp and lethargic and heavy at this point, because he was an enormous cat. She snatched the pillow out from under him, and threw an old sheet over the chair before replacing Chin on the cushion. After some gentle stroking, she disappeared with the pillow, probably to sterilize it with soap and water.

      It took a long time for Chin to recover. The hair on his neck returned somewhat darker as it had on my leg some months before, and within a season or so for my Chinny to return to normal, or almost! He was a bit of a mystery, and although we were of the same breed, give or take a little, I always had a feeling that, although he was savvy, he was a loner. One of his delights was to be thrown over a human shoulder. You could see him relish this position, his long limbs falling over, front and back, stretching on both sides. He'd cuddle lovingly then suddenly tighten up with a jerk to imply he'd had enough. There was nothing to do but to let him go. Off he'd scramble with other things to do, time to get on with it.

It was late April. The weather was now clear, and warm enough for us all to stay outside. We were a bit temperamental, Chin and I. Sometimes we would go our separate ways, but because spring had begun to appear, we spent much of our time sunning and watching insects take flight. Hiiyah began gaining weight to the point where Missy was told to reduce her daily portion by half and to monitor her diet. She continued to grow fat, resembling a stuffed sausage, which repulsed everyone. One day, I decided to follow her to discover where she was going to supplement her diet. It wasn't long before Missy discovered this, too, as she witnessed her eating the fresh manure from the horses in the field. I wouldn't have been surprised if I were to find that "our girl" had disappeared, leaving Huuwah a single dog down home on this range. We would have been far better friends if and when that day had come, I can assure you.

A long time passed with normal activity taking place on the DO OH DA AH Ranch when, one morning, Missy came running into the house before she could even fix our breakfast, with the news that we had a new colt.

Shaella, the black, had given birth near the shed on a full moon night. Missy was beside herself. Everyone got their things on and bolstered up some fresh morning energy to follow Missy to our future race horse! I'm sorry I missed that one. That's what happens sometimes when you're too comfortable, sleeping with your folks, nice and warm through the night. Later, though, as Chin and I peered down on him from the nearby railing, I found him sweet and beautiful, and certainly jet black like his parents. Not able to take my eyes from him as he stood still slightly wobbling next to his mother, I watched him nuzzle up to her for a drink of fresh, warm milk. We had been there a long time observing the new colt, when we were plucked from the fence and taken back with the rest where I, too, was feeling the pangs of breakfast time.

Being born on the first of May, it was only fitting that our new colt be given the name May Day which also gave one the feeling that he was going to be a runner like his dad; a shot in the dark, a grand prix type. He was given a lot of attention and was watched by all of us for several weeks until, one afternoon, quite suddenly, Sophie was coming into labor in broad daylight. I could hear her whinny and sensed she was not happy so I dashed to the fence to check on her. No one was around. Everyone was gone. I didn't like what I saw as Sophie lay there on the ground wreathing in pain. My, that looked difficult. Somehow I'm glad I didn't have to put up with that after all. As she lay there, she continued to struggle to give birth. Oh, I wish there was something I could have done! Then, suddenly, there was a noise at the back gate.

Fibby had appeared in his car unexpectedly and was beckoned by Missie who had just returned herself. Then Rennie arrived from school and joined the others now in the pasture. I had to lean a bit to see around the corner but sat there waiting quietly. They didn't need to worry about me; I had a ringside seat. Anyway, I always made sure of that, for that was all I could do, of course, just watch. Missy ran into the house to get the camera while Rennie and Fibby went to assist Sophie. When Missy appeared, I could see flashes and Fibby pulling something from Sophie. Rennie helped Fibby and by golly, there was all of a sudden, another little colt on the field. The three of them were busy, I could see that, and then once the foal was clean, Missy picked him up and hugged him as though he was only a few pounds. Fibby and Rennie stood back, relieved they had come home when they did for Missy could never have delivered this foal alone.

What excitement! There's just no end to it here! It almost wears me out thinking about it. Sophie's foal was quite unlike May Day for he was red, a beautiful rusty red, and his freshness gleaned in the sunlight. Also strong and healthy, he was quite a contrast to his jet-black brother. Having long, slender legs, and a spirited personality, he was given the name of Roo for Kanga Roo in Christopher Robin. The "boys" were very different as they grew. Only two weeks apart, they were great companions and playful brothers. I loved to watch them from the fence post. Each day I'd find some time to climb the post and sit there watching them swish their tails, communicating with one another, dashing about the back forty to exercise their growing legs and nibble on the sparse grass. Yes, they'd just hang out while they were growing.

When the colts were still very young, I remember one particular morning, an especially clear and sunny day when Missy was spending extra time with the them. She had a tendency to treat us all as her own children, and as I sat on the fence post, I found her sitting on the ground between the colts, who were lying head-to-head in the warm Sun. Much to my surprise, I watched her gently place their heads in her lap, before she began caressing them and singing to them. They apparently enjoyed the attention, and perhaps the music, as they lay there in complete bliss. They say that if you pick up a newborn colt, they will always be trusting, and I believe that, because these boys would like to have talked, as would I. I knew the feeling.

I cannot help but remember an incident, which happened a few months later when the "boys" were getting very frisky and accustomed to the schedules at the ranch. May Day had found a way to tease Missy by rushing to the gate at the large hay and feeding shed while she was latching the gate near their exercise ring. While she was latching one, he was unlatching the other, which gave him the freedom to run out to the grass at the four corners. He would get to the center and turn around to look at her, smug and pleased for outsmarting Missy. I could tell she was amused, but realizing it could get out of hand, she put a double latch on the other gate to get even with him.

Sometime ago, one of the corrals had been turned into a chicken stall. A rooster and some hens had been delivered, which really got my goat sometimes. Birds are so dirty! Actually, we had two roosters. The first one was very nasty and seemed to enjoy pecking the ladies to the point where they were losing their feathers and running around looking naked. He was replaced with a more kindly one who would crow early in the morning and wake me out of a deep sleep. Who wants to wake up that early? My tummy doesn't begin to rumble until seven o'clock, but certainly not at five when the sun begins to rise here. The black Anacondas laid large green eggs. I was even offered one but I couldn't stomach it and walked away. I didn't hang around that stall very much for I didn't really appreciate the constant aggravating noise of the cackling hens. There were red hens as well who sat clucking as they lay in their nests in the coop. Soon there was an abundance of eggs in every nest, so many I couldn't count them all.

Then, for some reason, the happy hens began to die. They were usually found dead in the morning at feeding time. This was quite a mystery until one morning Missy found out why. Hiyaah had somehow made her way through a camouflaged break in the chicken fence and began to attack them, one by one. By then, everyone considered her as the menace on the premises. In desperation, Missy found an old timer who suggested that she tie a dead chicken around the dog's neck for three days, adding... 'that would change her nasty habit!' Well, you can just imagine what that looked like and how badly she smelled in those three days. As I've alluded earlier, I didn't like her from the beginning and steered clear of her as best I could. Thank heavens I could climb out of her reach when it became necessary once in a while and that I didn't have to sleep with her, especially during her punishment. We only had two sets of chickens before Missy and Hubby decided it was a useless venture. What a relief that was! At the time, there were twenty-one mouths to feed several times in a single day. Now it would relieve Missy of at least one of her chores.

Fall was a favorite time of mine when the colors would be so vivid, even to me who was supposed to be colorblind! We cats will surprise you every now and then, you know. I have to admit that the animals here on the ranch did get nervous during the hot air balloon festival. There were times when these balloons got just a little too close for my comfort, especially when they made a habit of landing on our property during the festivities. The hissssssssing noises induced most of us to find shelter, preferably in the house. The hounds would go crazy, baying frantically as they sought cover under someone's bed. These balloons can be very loud and scary as they slowly approach. Then, almost as quickly as they appear, they're off again.

Winter was beautiful on the ranch. The watermelon color on the Sandia Mountain was a favorite sight for me so I would sunbathe out on the banco to watch the snow light up. I remember vividly one particular night when it snowed, turning the valley into a fairyland. By morning, the crispy mist shimmered in the fresh air, hovering over several inches of snow. My master had come for a visit. That morning, he quietly got up, hoping he had not disturbed me, but I had my eye on him nevertheless and watched him gather his camera as he tiptoed to the door which he slipped through. I rose and leapt to the window to catch a glimpse of him outside. He was taking photographs of the shimmering light off the new snow as it gleamed from the rays of the climbing sun. He took many photos of our homestead, as it was disappearing now, enveloped by the pristine thickness of a new white blanket.

When my master, Roik, left for good, I moved back to the big house where I found comfort in being the matriarch, the lead feline if you will, and I made it quite clear that things would be best if they went my way. I was entirely spoiled because my master had taught me nothing else, and I took for granted that things wouldn't change; that my position would always remain as it was. With a few bumps and bruises, I think things went quite smoothly over the years.

Winter was the hardest on Missy who really had her hands full. Each morning she would feed the outside animals before tending to the rest of us indoors, but winter was more difficult because she had to break the ice in the water trough and haul water from the house because the outdoor pipe was inevitably frozen. She would scoop out the delicious barley and molasses oats to add to the hay where the horses waited patiently beside her. Because they had kept a few chickens through the winter, she would duck into the coop to throw out their grain, check the water, and collect the fresh eggs, if there were any.

We had an exceptional harvest that late spring from our fruit trees. Rennie made enough plum wine and jam to hold us for a long while. Of course, I didn't enjoy the 'fruits' of these labors, but I could enjoy everyone "ooing" and "ahing" over them. That was not exactly what pussycats like anyhow, so I didn't miss a thing.

One morning as we were having breakfast, Rennie's new friend, Brooze, noticed a pretty little orange tabby cat sitting in the wisteria vine on the arbor in the back yard. I went to the windowsill and wondered who he was, too, for I had never seen him on the premises, and wondered how he got there. He was meowing to get someone's attention all right, so I sat there for some time giving him full inspection. Because the "tabby" had the color of a penny, they called him Henny Penny and he instantly became an addition to our family. He was a lot bigger than Chinny and me and had long hair. He had very large, green eyes, and hind feet that resembled those of a jack rabbit.

Missy sat at her desk quite often to take care of the menial tasks of running the ranch. She wrote a lot there in her little study near the back door where she could see anyone who might be coming in the gate or generally keep an eye on things on that side of the house. I would find comfort in sitting under her lamp as she did her work there.

May Day and Roo were growing fast now and someone, usually Missy or Hubby, would walk them each day around the block. Hubby loved the exercise and, once being a cowboy on a large cattle ranch for a summer with his brother, he loved to ride and was anxious to take the boys, nearly two now out for a spin. They were so nice and playful, but as they got larger, they moved into the terrible two's, which never happened to me! You know, when a two-year-old wants everything his/her way, he/she can really feel the growing pains to the point of disruption. The boys, sometimes with their mothers, were let out frequently now to run in to the large front lawn where they caught the eye of drivers passing by as the large property was on a corner where two country roads crossed. Some even stopped to take pictures because it was so pretty there, they said. Missy spent her waking hours gardening and trying to make the place picture perfect, but she could have used my help. The trouble was I knew I was too small, so I'd gather Chinny and Henny Penny and we'd follow her around to keep her company. Another cat soon appeared out of the blue whom we called "Nubie" for Nubian. He was as black as the Ace of Spades and from whence he came no one knew. He was enormous with great, green eyes, and he was easy to get along with as well.

It wasn't long before Jedd brought Missy a small, white, longhaired kitty. It seems a friend of his had a cat who had given birth to kittens some weeks before and as he watched the litter grow, they were all spoken for but one. The last of the litter needed a home, so he decided not to leave him behind. He put the wee thing in a box and brought him to Missy as a surprise. Oh, how I remember when her eyes lit up as she picked up the tiny, irresistible longhaired white kitten, stealing her heart away. There was no other name for him but Chris Kringle who we all referred to as "Kringle," ne Kringy Ringy Dingy from that moment on. His favorite sleeping habit was on his back, with legs stretched out to fall away in complete bliss, between the back of the sofa and cushion, exposing his adorable pink tummy through the soft white fur. In time, he grew to be another large cat. He had great green eyes and spent most of his time with Nubie, who became his mentor. They were almost inseparable. Black and white, quite a sight!

We felines were all compatible and had good times together. We'd sit out in the back patio at the entrance to the back door. There were some rattan chairs surrounded by a low adobe wall with slate on top for sitting and with a corbelled overhang in the roof above. By then the number of saucers had grown to five at the feeding station beside the sink on the long kitchen counter, which made it easier for Missy to feed us all at once. We just ate in our cat corner and kept quiet. Once our meal was over, we'd scatter to bathe in our own privacy before resuming our lifestyles.

One thing I noticed about Kringle was that he loved water which I had fun watching him play in. Not bathe in, mind you, just paw and play. Sometimes I would sit on the edge of the bathtub and watch him climb in with Missy who filled it only an inch or two when he was there keeping her company.

Chinny's health suddenly began to fail and I guess he died of that terrible mishap. This made me very sad. Quite by accident, Missy found him very stiff one morning beside Jedd's bed where I suppose he had lain quietly to die, nearly hidden from the rest of the world. My guess is that Chinny never completely recovered from his illness, which we thought Rennie had cured with her attentive TLC. We buried him in the garden and made a little cross above him.

Meanwhile, the "boys" were growing very large and scared me a bit when they raced about. May Day got some sort of infection which needed tending to so Hubby brought home a large syringe with penicillin, which he had to give him in the rump. Hubby needed help from Missy so I went out to give them moral support. It wasn't easy to corral this oversized colt, and I felt like closing my eyes and looking away at times as I watched them rope him to the post for Missy to hold him steady in order for Hubby to plunge the large needle into his hip. We all knew that May Day would never want to hurt either of them, but being a colt not feeling too well, he didn't like the looks of that needle either, and swung around forcing Missy to fall into the dowels of the feeding rack. Holding tight to the rope as the needle went into his rump, Missy broke two dowels. Luckily, it wasn't her back instead! Every now and then I shudder a little when I remember this incident. May Day recovered, never to be sick again to my knowledge.

There was a good deal of excitement that following autumn when the leaves were just beginning to turn. Brooze and Rennie were getting married and while sitting nearby and very still, I could hear the family discussing their plans. Rennie wanted the wedding at the house, under the large cottonwood tree in the sheltered garden near the old Spanish wall, smothered with large topieried junipers. They thought the walk through the old wooden gate past the large multi-paned window in the grand living room would be the path to take. After the date was set, Hubby rented a tent where his band, the ABQ Jazz, would play. The bridesmaids would wear Liberty print dresses which Rennie made herself with measurements coming through the mail. She made Missy's dress as well. Out-of-town guests came from far away; some stayed at the ranch, while others found nearby hotels. The big day a day I will remember, one where I could have been trampled on easily had I not had the sense to perch in high places, almost unnoticed. One can see more, too, I always thought.

I really don't know how Missy was able to keep up with all of us and get the ranch looking the way she wanted it by the end of September, the time of year when a gardener is putting the gardens to sleep. Rennie was finishing school and sewing madly upstairs on her machine where the parrots would watch with concentration, moving occasionally with an occasional squawk as they stood on their perches. I'd sit on the end of her bed snuggled into her folded comforter and feeling oh so comfortable, able to take in the view of the entire back garden where she would be wed.

People began to arrive the day before the big day, and the bustle was exciting. They were always eating, it seemed! We woke the next morning on a clear sunshine day, the wedding day, which, of course delighted everyone. It was going to be a glorious event. Rennie had been hiding from Brooze, which is custom, I've heard, and Hubby was looking fine in his tuxedo, prepared for the moment to walk his only daughter to the grand old cottonwood tree. As I remained upstairs with the parrots watching at the window from Rennie's room, I could see the guests begin to arrive with umbrellas and raincoats, prepared for anything as they gathered into the garden. The bridesmaids walked through the rustic door from the front patio and down the meandering brick path, lined with raised fresh flower baskets, to join the ushers already standing with the bride and groom under the tree. It became calm and quiet. I could hardly hear what the minister was saying as it was, but then, to make matters worse, a helicopter we had never seen before appeared in the sky above the tree. There it was, grinding out its noise while it stirred up a bit of wind for what seemed like a few minutes before disappearing. All of a sudden, the sun went behind a cloud and it began to hail. It was a very peculiar day for September in

Albuquerque. As the weather became more difficult, the minister just kept talking down there. Everyone became "teary-eyed" as he tried rapidly to finish the "I do's" so that the guests could run for cover when the heavens really opened up. What timing! There was a mad dash for the spacious living room, which Hubby and Rennie's brothers were now emptying as fast as they could.

A mess to be sure, but one that everyone overlooked, remembering that such weather always brought good luck to the bride and groom. Hubby's band began to make music at the end of the large living room near the piano by the windows facing the inner garden. The guests had come indoors from the nasty weather and were dancing for quite awh until the time came for Brooze and Rennie to be driven away out the front gate. For the most part, our family life returned to normal in a day or two for the menagerie and the immediate family at the DO OH DA AH Ranch.

Our life continued for nearly a year when something happened at the ranch, which was disturbing to all of us, almost as though someone had died. We felt edgy. I couldn't quite put my paw on it but for some reason I had a hunch things would begin to change. Well, things did change. Rennie and Brooze moved away, and Fibby married Sooz and moved to another part of town. Then a man came by with his small children, put Huuwah and Hiyaah into a car and disappeared out of the back gate. I didn't miss Hiyaah, which was actually a blessing, but I must admit I had mixed emotions about Huuwah, as I had fond memories of the times we all sat outside in the small protected adobe back porch with low walls for sitting on just passing the time, knowing all was well; that we would be fed on time and cuddled each day, perhaps even given a brush now and then. We cats purred a lot during those times.

Jedd had already been gone for sometime. Apparently, he had moved to New York City and took his colorful orange V-Dub with him. Nubie had loved to sit on top of the bug from time to time for quiet time I would guess, and after awhile, he'd rise and arch his back which made his tail curl. Someone took a photo of him one year at Halloween during this pose which Missy used for a Halloween card. Jedd was always dashing about like a free spirit. I hated to see him go because he was responsible for bringing Kringle into the family fold and he had a cheerful, bellowing voice which rang out upon his arrival.

Then, the next thing I knew, a man I'd never seen before picked up Nubie and Henny Penny and he, too, sped away, out the gate. Oh, dear, I didn't even have a chance to say goodbye. I never saw Nubie again.

Without much notice, Missy and Hubby left and Rennie and Brooze moved back to the homestead temporarily to live in the "batch." They had a dog, Dinah, who was big and black with too much energy. She really had liked to chase the feline population occasionally on visits, which was alright, but when she moved in with Rennie and Brooze, I wasn't sure I'd like that. My peaceful state of mind was becoming somewhat frazzled now and I didn't like this period of time in my life. With my master gone and Missy and Hubby having left, and with new people coming and going, there was not much continuity in our lives anymore. I was also lonesome for Nubie and Henny Penny.

Rennie and Brooze cared for the horses now. Roo and May Day were very tame and still amused me sometimes as I sat quietly on the fence watching them play and whinny, kicking up their heads and tails. On occasion, they even poked their heads in the windows of the "batch" to watch television. They seemed almost mesmerized during the French Open Tennis Tournament one beautiful day, and lingered on at the window for some time, I thought. They took great delight in running full speed, completely around the fenced-in area.

Hubby and Missy's absence really put a void in our lives, those of us who were left that is. I found it very difficult for awhile, but the incident pulled those of us still remaining closer together, I suspect.

It was some nine months later when the horses left. Kringle and I were put in the car with Rennie and Brooze to be taken to a faraway place. I was very nervous, almost as jittery as I am when I'm being taken to the vets for my yearly check-up. Henny Penny had meanwhile found his way back across town to Rennie, but stayed at the ranch until the final move. Only Kringle and I were transported to the city of Springfield, Illinois, where Missy and Hubby were now living.

 I never dreamed of living in a hotel, the Hilton Hotel, but Kringle and I learned to be careful that we were not found living there. We could sit at the window and look down at Lincoln's Historic Street from the seventeenth floor. Occasionally, if the door was ajar, we'd scamper out into the empty hall to explore, not too sure about the elevator, but for the most part we would behave. Kringle was feistier than I, and would dart about giving Missy a start, but he never did anything wrong except sneak into the elevator once or twice, which kept Missy a little nervous.

 It wasn't until one year later when we moved into the country, more like where we had come from, and it was here that life would change completely for all of us. We would learn the dangers of water and other invading animals because everything here was open. We would feel the seasons, which sometimes gave Hubby hay fever, making him sneeze and sneeze. All this eventually settled down and we became accustomed to our new home, which became known as the "Sows Ear." Hubby's German name means wild boar or "little wild boars" and one hot day Missy was so tired after sanding floors that she named the three acres "Sows Ear," hoping someday after renovation, it would be a "silk purse," whatever that meant! Quietly sheltered between a lake and the golf course on a dead-end street, we had a lot of territory to discover.

 Hubby and Missy worked hard on the little bungalow facing westward towards the lake on one side, and across the open acres filled with large old trees to the golf course. It took several years to convert the bungalow into a home that fit the family lifestyle. I watched them planning, building additions, laying brick walks, and creating a slate patio backed by a trellis Hubby had built which was eventually covered with wildly growing purple wisteria. Missy planted another white wisteria she had brought with her from Albuquerque which she pruned to resemble an umbrella that bloomed twice a year. I remember watching them standing high on scaffolds, shingling the whole house themselves. The home grew and grew. Sometimes I got lost, but when the renovations were complete and all the workmen were gone, we learned our way around and became ultimately comfortable finding many little niches to sleep in.

Kringle was my best friend now; really like a little brother to me. He became my ward, but then, from the beginning, I was thought of as the old sage, and he knew that when I gave him a puckered, old maid look, one of austere supremacy, a characteristic of my breed, my expression made it perfectly clear where I stood on matters. I didn't mean to appear fearsome, but it just came across that way quite naturally, I'm afraid. I loved being the matriarch and took the responsibility for my clan as best I could. On occasion Kringle would go down to the water's edge where he would sit quietly in fascination on a low rock looking like a miniature polar bear as he'd watch the fish moving and jumping close by, darting along the shore beside the riprap. Without so much as a quiver, he would, with natural finesse, thrust his paw out and flip his jumping fish over onto the grass beside him and proceed to demolish his delectable. Kringle was an imp. Though attentive and oh so lovable, he could misunderstand his own strength from time to time and forget he had claws on his feet. All was overlooked, for Kringle could do no wrong and Missy told him so in many ways.

Our life changed again somewhat when a big, burly man moved next door with his two large black dogs. I thought they deserved one another, but in fact the dogs were nicer than the man. I was feeling helpless outside anymore and stayed indoors more than I wanted. One never knew where or when those dogs would come from, sniffing about.

Missy became very anxious too, and I began to see a change in her. She was nervous, careful about the doors, and rarely left us alone. Early in the morning, the man would walk his dogs around the house. Their snuffles would wake us and we'd be at the windows, watching their every move. They had indeed invaded our privacy, which made us feel vulnerable. We never knew when we might find him looking in the windows as well. His little children would come over and romp around also without any feeling of invading our territory. They didn't live there so they weren't around that much. Missy and Hubby put up a long, split-rail fence, which was meant to keep them out. The trash men stopped coming back to the house also, and so they no longer frightened us.

When Jedd left New York City, we adopted Chelsea. Missy called her Chelly Welly. She had lots of fleas, which she brought with her to share with the rest of us. I don't ever remember having fleas, even at the ranch, but Missy had to take the time to deflea us almost daily. She'd sit against the bathroom sink with hot water running and put a comb through our coats to clean out the masses of the annoying critters before running them through the hot water and down the drain. It wasn't long before we stopped scratching and felt less stress, but I must admit I missed the combing for it felt delicious, like a treat. We had all decided it was something to look forward to. Chelly was not an easy cat. She had a habit of waiting around the corner to pounce on us, especially Kringle. She'd stir up a fuss, which made our little imp nervous. Any play between us would find Chelly running to get into the fun, but instead she'd ruin our play and we'd have to postpone it altogether. She was a type of calico, black and white, which put her in a lower rung of the ladder in the cat world. She just didn't fit in.

When Rennie and Brooze moved to Texas, they brought Henny Penny to join us on their next visit because Dinah, their black lab, was all they could handle at the time. As I might have said before, Henny was an orange tabby who had been sent away with Nubie, but he miraculously returned to the ranch some months later to find Rennie. I guess he was especially fond of her. He was kind of schizoid from the beginning, but he was a sweet fellow whose enormous eyes could show his emotional sensitivity. I think someone must have been very cruel to him, for every time he heard a heavy foot, he'd stop dead in his tracks. His green eyes would grow wide and he would simply freeze or moved away quickly. He and Kringle got along just fine, but Chelsea really made things difficult for the boys, especially. She would dash to a door where Henny waited to enter and intimidate him, not allowing him to pass. It took someone to interfere so that he could even move toward his dish at suppertime.

Kringle loved to sit at the desk under the warmth of the light while Missy was working there. Chelsea would interrupt him and once again try to intimidate him. He became very nervous around her and simply left to find a place away from her. Missy would hug him madly or throw him over her shoulder, as she did with all of us. He found her enormously comfortable all snuggled up in her arms, particularly while she slept at night. He would lie on his back along one of her legs, deliciously smothered in the coverlet; then in the middle of the night he would cuddle with me at the foot of the bed.

I remember the very large American flag hanging over the deck railing. One day it was blown over the railing to lie draped on the deck still attached but now lying on the deck, providing a sort of hammock. Kringle found this a comfy place to lie, feet up. It was an unforgettable moment. Missy ran for the camera only to find him gone by the time she returned to immortalize the pose. His humor was contagious and he was delightful to be around.

One day, early in the morning, large trucks and machines drove into the next-door lot and tore down the little house. The burly man and his dogs disappeared, and our life regained some freedom. Every now and then Kringle and I would go over to the empty lot to explore the flora and fauna, the peaceful area left where the house had been. The burly man returned occasionally in his little red pick-up to inspect what might have been his, but instead, he was informed he could no longer visit the property because it belonged to someone else now. Occasionally we would find a chipmunk to catch that we'd take to the back door for Missy. Sometimes the head would be delicious but only if we were especially hungry. Birds also amused us and occasionally we'd get scolded when we caught one.

There was one thing we cats all had in common and that was a torn ear. I suppose, during an occasional battle, we would rarely escape without a scratch of some kind. When I was younger, I didn't have the sense sometimes to step back and let differences be ignored. Instead, I would stand my ground probably over something silly. Nevertheless, a torn left ear remained to blemish my appearance forever. Henny Penny's right ear was torn when he arrived. Kringle was most likely the culprit for the damage to Chelly Welly's right ear. I must say, though, that Kringle's left ear which had been torn when he was little grew rather distinguished as little white hairs grew long on the tip.

That winter when Missy and Hubby left town, a nice old man came to stay with us. On the day of their return, Kringle was nowhere to be found. Missy suspected that he had not been feeling well and simply had gone off to die somewhere but, after an extensive search for him, she began to wonder if that burly man next door hadn't stolen him. Anything could be possible with that man! She had always suspected he took her colorful Arabic carpet drying on the front brick walk or the large yellow pipe-smokers crosswalk sign which had been given to Hubby who wanted to show it off at the roadside. She called everyone she could think of who might know what happened to her beloved cat. None of the vets, or anyone else, for that matter, had an inkling of Kringle's whereabouts. I think her heart was broken and I tried to soothe her pain. He was special to me, too, and I'm afraid I moped around as well for a good long time. Oh, I did miss that Kringle, or as Missy used to call him, Kringie Ringie Dingie.

About a year later, a new house was built next door on the empty piece of property where the burly man had lived temporarily. We'd pass the time by sitting on the split rail fence between the properties to watch the activity in progress. Once it was finished, a new family moved in with a new cat that looked much like Henny Penny, which was too bad because we had to look twice at times to make sure which cat was which. He was also neutered, but never allowed into his house, so he was just one more addition to the local population. I felt kind of sorry for him because I never did know his name and he looked dirty and lonely when he was fed beside their back step. I know, because I sauntered around the fence to acquaint myself with the new fancy home which Missy called the "Purrrfect House."

Once again, things changed for me because I did not feel as compatible with Henny, or Chelsea in particular. It took a long time to understand Henny, who eventually became some sort of a substitute friend. He was more my age, or, maybe a year younger. He was lean, with a beautiful orange coat and white tail with a crook at the end from having been broken at some time or another. He resembled a tiger, I think. Chelsea, on the other hand, was out of sorts with the rest of us from the beginning, fitting into the "third wheel" category. Suddenly, a rather large, dark brown and black calico began to visit, almost too often, in my opinion. His goal seemed to be to get into the house for a free meal and he would do his darnedest to do so. Missy became aware of this and kept an eye on the doors. She even closed the garage doors, which earlier had been raised ever so little, just enough for us felines to come and go as we pleased. Having the door closed now became a bit of a strain on all of us, but Missy thought this might keep the interloper from prowling around altogether. He wasn't visiting me, that's for sure! It was quite obvious that he and Chelsea seemed enamored with one another. For spells at a time, he could be seen sleeping on the chaise chair on the veranda in the morning and every so often, he came to the door with a wild yowl hoping we would include him in our family activities.

I suppose another reason for keeping the garage door down was because of the raccoons and 'possums that, on occasion, would sneak in uninvited to enjoy the comfort of our home. One day when we were all left alone, we watched an opossum come in and hide in the living room. Missy returned home from school to study. Aware of our intruder, we were all perched in separate areas of the big room when she picked up her books and took them to the window seat where she often studied. She would prop up the pillows and sit in the corner with good natural light. On this particular occasion, we watched her with interest because we weren't too sure what would happen when she puffed up the pillows before snuggling into them. As we had suspected, she saw the long, white, slender tail, but when she pulled the pillow away, she was surprised to find an opossum that lifted his head, disturbed from his nap in the darkness, and hiss at her. We were all surprised when she calmly put the pillow back against him where she found it. A man came later to pick him up and take him away, but it happened again, at which time Hubby found a piece of PC pipe, doubled a cord before threading the pipe to make a loop which he quickly wrapped around the varmint's neck before taking it somewhere outside. The raccoon, however, was quite a different story, as she made herself at home by climbing the ladder in the garage and working her way through the insulation where she proceeded to have her brood just above the kitchen near a ceiling light. Once again, a man came to the rescue and took them all away.

Over the years, I have been called the "musical cat" because I love to dance while being held in someone's arms. My master held me and sang to me when I was little which helped me appreciate a little quick step now and then. Missy would invariably swing around with a bounce while holding me, then she'd throw me up on my back, holding my derriere in the air, and continue singing and swinging while carrying me through a cake walk. I sang, too, the only way I knew how, which was a high "Yeow!" I meant it to sound as though I was squealing with delight and I hope that's what she thought it was, too, because I just loved the attention. Everyone loves attention. It's very important for one's ego. She tried to make us all purr each day which is also good for the digestion, they say.

One afternoon during the new spring, one year later, Kringle was accidentally found in the loft of the garage. He was in a box in the far corner sitting up in a frozen state, staring, eyes wide open. We were so astonished to think that he was there all that time without our knowing it. Missy climbed the ladder and brought him down, box and all, to wrap him up for burial. She and Hubby took him down to the lower garden near the water to bury him and planted a Delaware white azalea above his grave to immortalize him properly. It was a sad day, I thought.

We all loved to follow Missy as she went to work in the garden. Sitting back on our haunches nearby, we kept her company, taking delight in watching the small, mischievous movements all around us. After the house was finished, she spent hours planting and changing things, clearing out brush, designing new areas, and adding split rail fences. During a family gathering, everyone took a turn digging out a long, narrow creek, which meandered from the road to the lake. We used to love to watch the water ripple around the subtle corners and under the small bridges that Hubby built. Why, the grounds became so beautiful with flowering trees and shrubs that the time came when she decided to change the name from "Sow's Ear" to "EBERPARK," and a park it was.

Time has passed, and having turned sweet sixteen on August twentieth, I want to make it purrrfectly clear that multiplying my age by seven, using the feline chart, makes me the eldest cat, giving me a definite edge as Queen of Hearts at Eberpark. Unfortunately, my eyes have gone bad, I'm afraid. My cataracts make it difficult for me to be in the sunlight or to see my surroundings the way I used to, therefore, I am a bit timid about getting into an open area that I may not be familiar with. I tend to sleep a great deal more to pass the time, which helps me to forget my arthritis that prevents me from getting around with a more youthful agility. I find it really taxing to get into the tub where I simply love Missy or Hubby to turn on the water ever so lightly so that I can watch it trickle down the drain. I often drink the water straight from the faucet instead of the bowl near our food dishes, or wash my face once in a while. Sometimes, I try to stay above at the faucet itself where I can lick from the spout, but I really find it easier anymore to relax at the bottom of the tub with a stream of water passing by. That way I don't feel rushed or grow tired in that awkward position where I am apt to get a nose full anyway.

The vet says I have something wrong with my kidneys so we are all on a special diet of Hill's Prescription K-D which we are given twice a day with a dab of Friskies meat or fish, especially for seniors, which makes it tastier. I just wish I didn't have the heaves every now and then because it wears me out and Missy has to clean up after me. It makes it particularly embarrassing when I lose my supper in the creases of the bed or on an oriental carpet. Without the tender loving care and respect for my needs, I probably wouldn't have lived this long what with all the stress over the years.

Whenever I see my master, who occasionally visits for several days at a time during the year, I instantly recognize his voice when he picks me up affectionately to cradle me in his arms, but it takes me a while to adjust to his presence. After all, I feel I must remind you that I'm a Seal Point Siamese and cautious by nature. He hasn't changed though, and I hope he never does because he is so sweet and gentle. Even though I have become almost blind, I can still recognize him for his great glimmering smile.

Now I have decided to take one day at a time. Each morning I wake feeling just a bit more arthritic than the day before and get frustrated when I can't see, but I do feel relieved when I hear the familiar voice of Missy and Hubby and can find my dish at mealtime.

Henny Penny and Chelly Welly have remained somewhat distant over these years. Oh, they Il sit on the porch together or on the foot of the bed together but for the most part I've often wondered if they ever had the kind of conversations Kringle and I had. Henny has been like a little brother to me so I understand him well enough. I just don't think Chelly ever learned how to play as a kitten. I understand she was bought in a shelter in New York City with a nasty black cat who probably taught her nothing but bad manners, but as of late, she appears to be responding to Missy's attention and seems to be loosening up a bit. Although we are all considered family, we cats have learned to recognize our space and tend to defend it. I just wish Henny, who is only a year or two younger than I, could learn to ignore Chelly's teasing, although I must say, I think she's trying to improve, and with our good example, how can she help it? She spends much time gardening with Missy and romps about catching flying objects. I think from the beginning, part of the difficulty has been that we are from such diverse breeds, all with a fierce sense of priority in our pecking order. All in all, it could have been worse, I'm quite sure.

Occasionally, Missy and Hubby leave us here alone to tend the house. A very nice lady comes twice a day during their absence to tend to our needs, water the plants, and to basically check on various things. Missy usually leaves an itinerary and instructions for the other two to remain outside between visits, leaving me alone now, which rather pleases me, especially when she leaves the radio on the music station. When they return, the routine is welcomed with familiar voices and noises missed when they are gone. I also have them to cuddle up to at night, which gives me warmth and a sense of security, particularly as my health has become more fragile. I love their comfortable surroundings. The other two usually find their places at the foot of the bed on the long piece of polar fleece placed over the eiderdown to prevent their cat hairs from soiling the bed cover. Whenever Hubby sits in his chair to read or to watch TV, he welcomes me at his side where I squeeze in beside him as he spoils me with constant affection, quite unconsciously while he's reading, which can be for hours at a time.

    I haven't had much time or energy to think about the past year as the seasons have come and gone and I have actually celebrated my eighteenth birthday. Sometime in the fall, however, I began to have trouble keeping any food down at all, and preferred to sleep, sit, or curl up over One of the floor heaters. Most of my exercise is seeking out water to quench my thirst throughout the day. Just before Thanksgiving, Missy took me to the vet again.

    This time the vet told her I would not live past Christmas as my kidneys were failing and I was losing weight quickly. I am also getting a bit irritable. Why, I even find it difficult to purr. Henny Penny and Chelly Welly disappeared during the big Thanksgiving celebration when all the family arrived to liven up the place for some four days, but Missy and Hubby decided to keep me home so that my master in particular and other members of the family could see me. I guessed it would be the last time so I was grateful.

    After several days of celebration, the house was quiet again. I began to ignore the breakfast call. I found Missy standing over me, putting her eyes close to mine urging me to respond, but

I could have cared less. She picked me up and carried me to my breakfast dish hoping I would get some nourishment, but I couldn't bear the smell of it and walked away. I was more interested in the water bowl nearby and all I could do with that was look at it, maybe put my nose on the water as if to smell it or perhaps play with the movement of it, but I couldn't drink a drop. I found the kitty litter box just around the corner but had no reason to use it other than to heave and heave producing nothing by now, which was exhausting.

That day passed and, in the morning, I did something Missy hadn't seen me do for a long while. I went to the door, which told her I wanted to go outside. Asking no questions, she opened it and I walked out to the porch. Something came over me that morning. I felt I had to make just one more trip down to the beach, now very large, as the water level had dropped many feet, which it does in winter anyway. It was a particularly lovely day I thought, but I wasn't exactly sure how far I could get so I mustered up all the energy I had and kept walking. I continued down the stairs, across the patio, and down the steep hill to the beach where I could mosey about and feel the cool sand between my toes. I sauntered out to the water's edge to smell the fishy aroma and to reminisce a moment before returning to the hill. Pausing occasionally, I knew this would be my last excursion. Struggling with the remainder of my journey, I forged ahead with determination. Preoccupied with happy memories, my last journey was accomplished with a surge of energy as I turned to what seemed like a formidable hill before me. Slowly I climbed, pausing occasionally to catch my breath, to rest my weary body. Now with only the stairs ahead of me, I found it necessary to take three steps at a time, resting in between. By the time I had reached the top stair, I was ready for a long winter's nap and found Missy at the door waiting. I lay in the warm sunshine for the rest of the day, there on the floor near the loveseat where Henny was "nesting." Chelly was curled up on the bed. It was a lovely and quiet afternoon until Missy picked me up and took me to the car.

As I sat in her lap, she drove to the vets, and I somehow knew my suffering would be over. I stretched as best I could to recognize anything at all. The moment she parked the car I knew where we were. It was particularly quiet inside the familiar animal hospital so I was immediately put on the scale where I sensed a hush of astonishment. I guess because I had wasted away to practically nothing. Oh, I felt terrible alright; weak and feeble, no longer embarrassed by my appearance. After some attention on the examining table, the vet took me to another room to give me a sedative, which, to everyone's surprise, it made me "y-e-o-w-l" quite loudly. When we returned to the room, I was immediately given to Missy who sang to me and squeezed me tight. As I began to doze off, I couldn't help but think of the special life I'd had, almost good enough to tell. But nobody would ever believe me! I could feel her playing with my tail, running her fingers down each bony vertebra, tweaking them playfully as she had done so many times in jest.

Always wishing to die in the loving arms of someone who had taken such good care of me, I found great comfort where I was and could only respond to my Missy's attention by giving my tail a quick flip or two as hard as I could until I could no longer. Now in a peaceful state, I could barely feel the last shot.

Pye died December 6, 1999 at 3:45 pm with the gentle assistance of Euthanasia.

www.ingramcontent.com/pod-product-compliance
Ingram Content Group UK Ltd.
Pitfield, Milton Keynes, MK11 3LW, UK
UKHW061623240426
12048UKWH00049B/1659

9 781778 830013